The Dandy, 4th December, 1937.

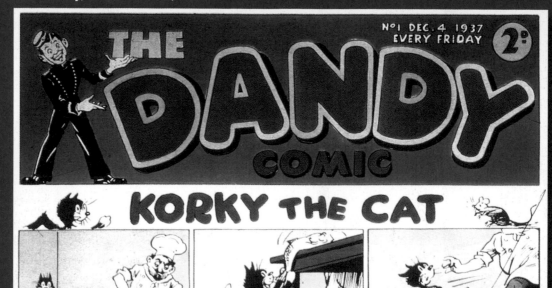

The Dandy is on sale every Wednesday.

Published by D C Thomson Annuals Ltd in 2012
DC Thomson Annuals Ltd, 185 Fleet Street, London EC4A 2HS
© D.C. Thomson & Co. Ltd. 2012

THE Dandy

1937 — 2012

75 years

Like most readers of The Dandy, I was introduced to comics by an older relative. An uncle of mine had a collection of Dandy comics and annuals, which he would produce whenever we visited. I loved the madcap incidents, larger-than-life characters and the sheer anarchy of it all. Most of all, I loved the fact that comics seemed to be NFG: Not For Grown-ups.

For this very special annual, we wanted to take characters from all periods of The Dandy's history, and recreate them for today. So whether you're an avid present-day Dandy reader (see you next Wednesday, guys!), or a lapsed reader reliving the comic of your youth, there's something in here for you.

Just don't let any grown-ups see your copy...

Craig Graham

The Dandy Editor

WINKER WATSON

Mr Creep bursts into the boys' dormitory at Greytowers School, home of the world's wiliest schoolboy wangler, Winker Watson...

BULLY BEEF and CHIPS

BLACK BOB THE DANDY'S WONDER DOG

Part One: Peace In The Valley

1 - A few short years after World War II, one man and his faithful sheepdog look out thoughtfully over the beauty of their homeland, admiring its great natural beauty, unchanged for centuries. Shepherd Andrew Glenn and Black Bob, his border collie sheepdog, had lived side by side through the dark times of war. And now, in peace, just one of the reasons why so many fought so bravely for their freedom lay before them. And within the safety of the valley's peace and tranquillity, they gave thanks.

2 - Suddenly, the peace was interrupted by the arrival of a large van, which parked nearby. "Ah, well - time we were getting home anyway, Bob," grinned Andrew.

3 - But before they turned for home, they were intrigued by what the new arrivals were doing, as they set about removing some impressive equipment from their van. "Nothing to be concerned about, sir," said one. "Just updating our maps of the area."

4 - But, as the pair began the journey home, Glenn spotted a small instrument lying in the road. "It must have fallen from their van. Take it back to them, Bob, and I'll see you back at the cottage. I'll have your dinner ready for you."

5 - Bob dutifully did as his master bid him, but something caught his eye as he left the instrument in the van. A model of a massive nuclear power station nestled right in the heart of the valley gave Bob cause for concern. His doggy mind decided all was not well here!

To be continued...

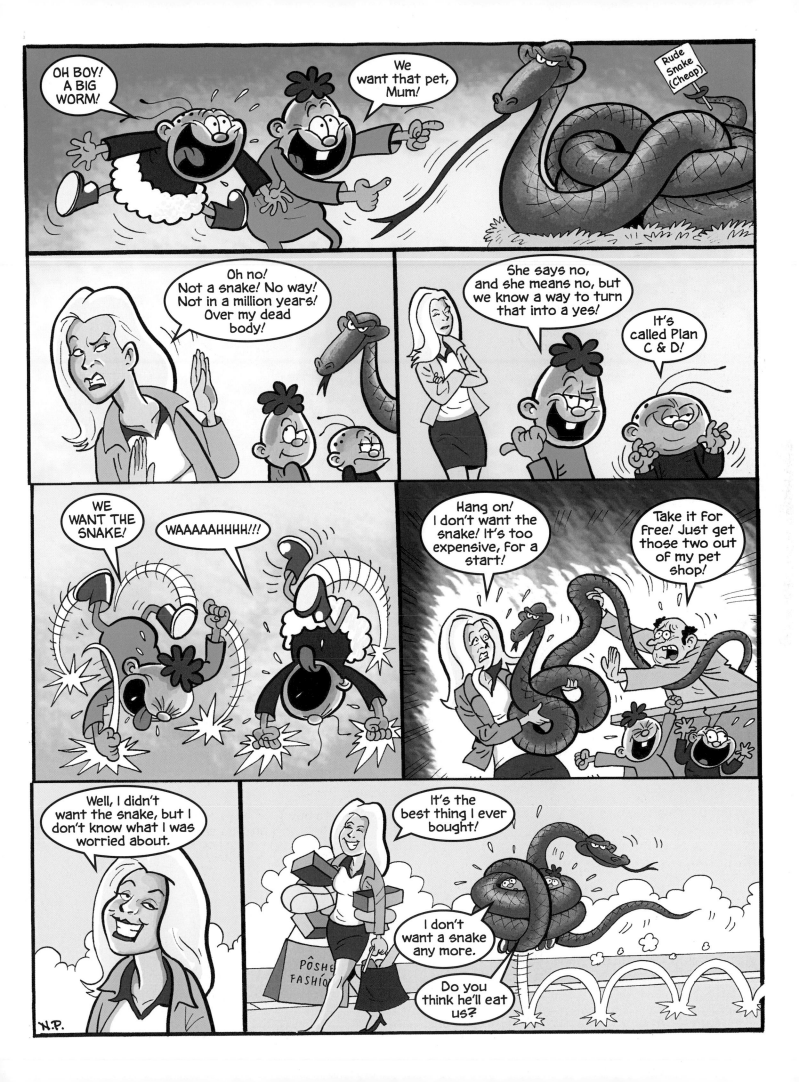

Beryl the Peril

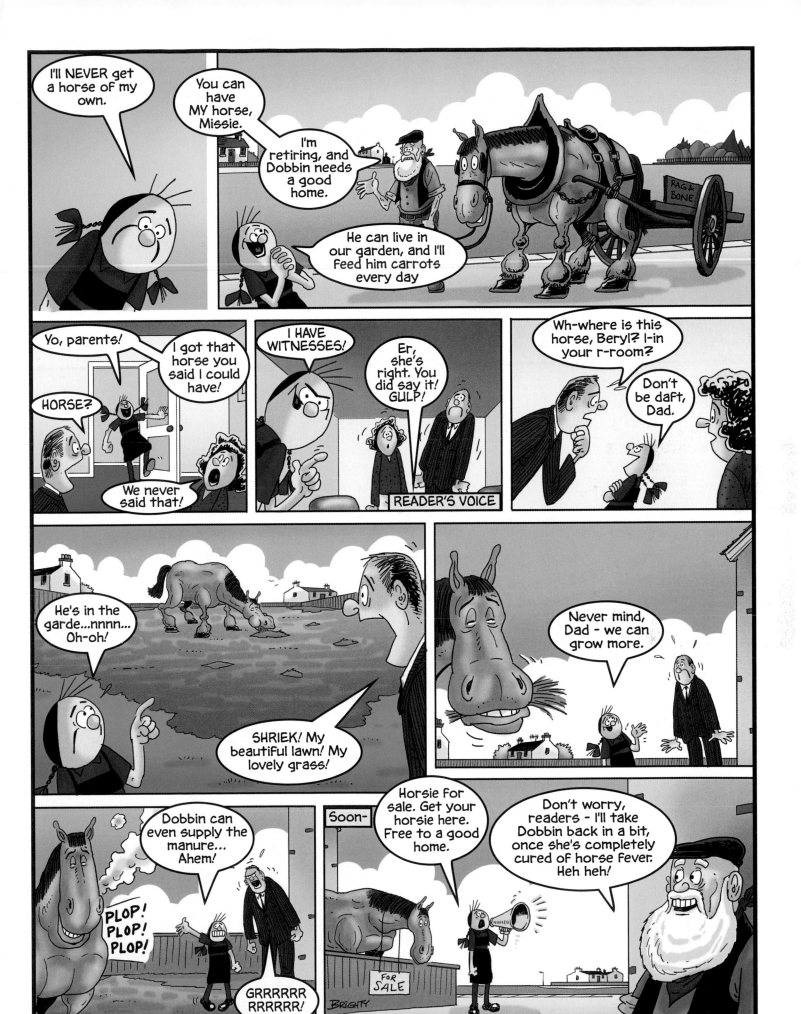

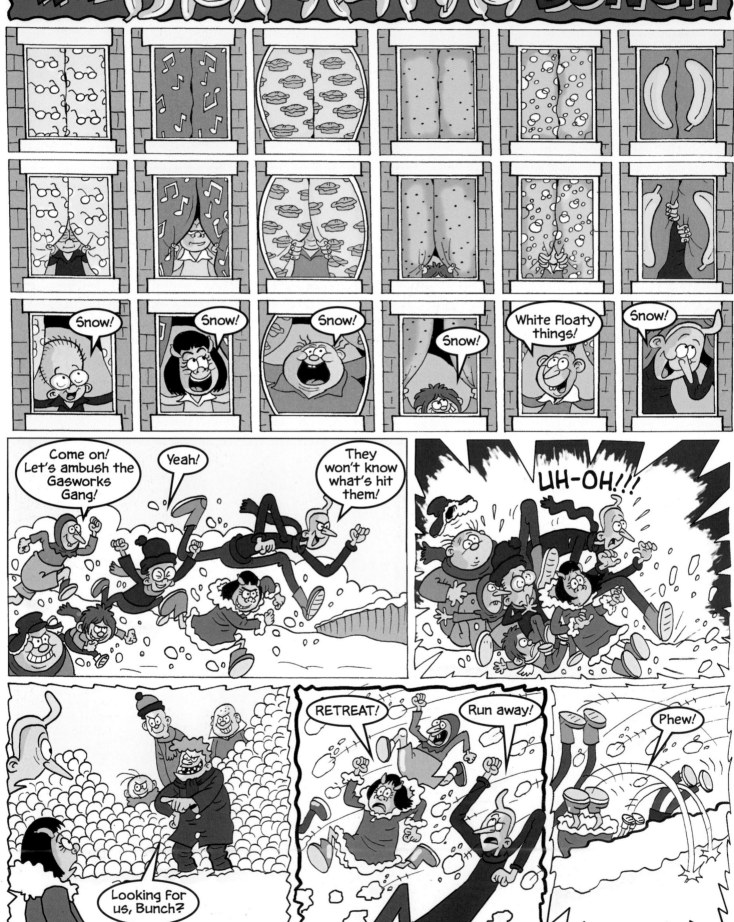

JULIUS SNEEZER THE SNEEZING CAESAR

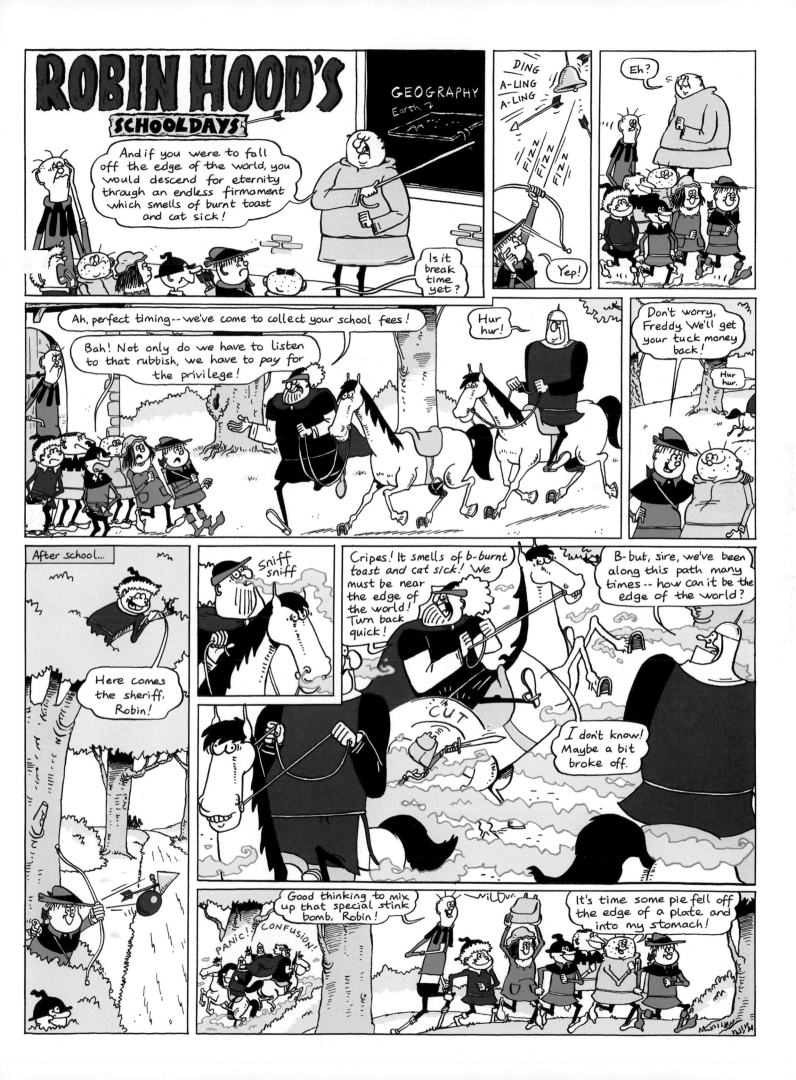

Monkey Bizness

PETER'S POCKET GRANDPA

It's blowing a gale outside, Grandpa!

Peter Parker's Grandpa once had an argument with a wizard, who shrank him to tiny size. Now, every day is an adventure for him!

Perfect for Flying a kite, Peter! Let's go!

Whoa! I'll be Flying too, at this rate!

Oh no! My cap!

I'll get it Grandpa!

Peter! Don't let go of the kite! You'll lose it!

Here Grandpa, I caught your hat...

Grandpa? Oh no! HANG ON, GRANDPA!

Don't worry, lad. I don't intend to let go!

Oh crikey, I'm getting higher and higher! Watchit, bird-brain!

BLACK BOB
THE DANDY'S WONDER DOG

Part Two: A Secret Uncovered

Black Bob has uncovered plans to build a nuclear power station in the valley...

1 - Instinctively, Bob decided to take some evidence back to his master. He grabbed a cardboard tube from the van and headed for home. But not before catching the eye of one of the suspicious workmen. "Hey, you!" called the man. "Bring that back!"

2 - Minutes later, Bob arrived home to be met by his master at the door, wondering what had taken the hound so long to get back for his meal. "*There* you are, Bob. Not like you to take your time when food is on offer. What's this you've brought me?"

3 - Andrew Glenn could hardly believe his eyes as he removed a large scroll of paper from the tube. He unfurled it before him on the table. "Crivvens, Bob!" he said, "It looks like a blueprint for a massive nuclear power station, right in the middle of our valley. Those men weren't mapping the area - they were measuring up the valley for this monstrosity."

4 - Andrew Glenn made a swift decision. There was no time to lose. The future peace and natural beauty of his beloved valley was at risk, and he wasn't about to stand idly by and let it happen. "I think the local press needs to hear about this, Bob," he said. Suddenly, there was an urgent knocking at the door.

5 - It was the workmen from the van. They looked worried and harassed. "We think your dog may have something of ours, sir. We'd like it back - now!" said one. Andrew Glenn wasn't about to play into their hands. "Dog?" he said, "Really? And what dog might that be?"

6 - Just then, Bob leapt out of the front window with the cardboard tube in his mouth, and raced off down the road. "Oh, you meant *that* dog!" grinned Andrew Glenn. "Run like the wind, Bob!" he called after the brave collie. "After him, Harry!" shouted the foreman. "Get in the van!"

To be continued...

THE Smasher

Angry Birds is my favourite game...

...'cos it's all about SMASHING things! Ha ha!

I think I'd be a Fantastic Angry Bird!

SMASH!

OW! Perhaps not with the catapult though!

Later...

STAGE DOOR

The local theatre gave me this old costume! Now for some smashing fun!

Meet SCOOTER JONES, a new character destined to have the shortest appearance in The Dandy Annual...

I'm SCOOTER JONES! I'm mad about scooters and my name's Jones.

That's my gimmick, my scooter.

It's why they call me SCOOTER JONES you see.

SQUAARK!

AAGH!

SMASH!

HA HA! They'll call you BROKEN Scooter Jones from now on!

Hey, it's a new gimmick. I can live with that.

Hey! That new bird's on our territory!

No way! There's already a shortage of worms around here and he's not getting ours!

PECK!

PECK!

PECK!

AAGH! GERROFF!

What's up, Smasher? I thought you LIKED angry birds?

LEW STRINGER

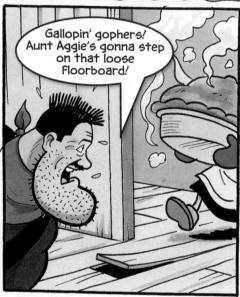

WINKER WATSON

The boys of Greytowers School Third Form are out cross-country running. They're not keen, but champion wangler Winker Watson is on the case...

The next day, in the boys' dormitory...

This is the sort of sport I like! In the warmth, for one thing.

CRACK

Shot, Trotty! You'll play for England one day.

Catch it, Pilchy!

SMASH!

Oops!

Now we're for it!

Don't worry, Lads. I'll think of something.

Got it! Boffy, can you find us a golf ball from somewhere? And Newty, can you keep a watch on Creepy's room and tell us when he's next practising his putting?

And so...

Everyone's in position, Trotty!

Good lad, Squinky!

Get ready...

Now!

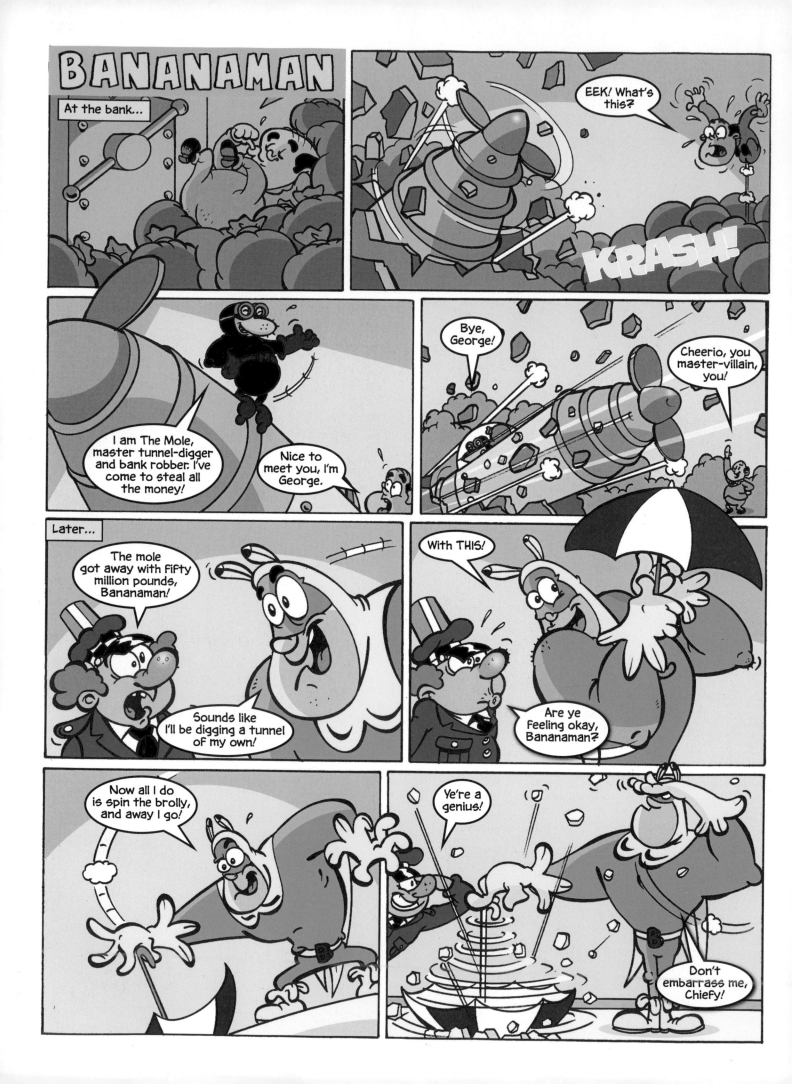

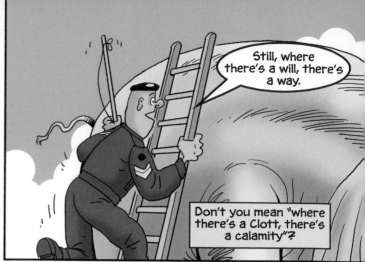

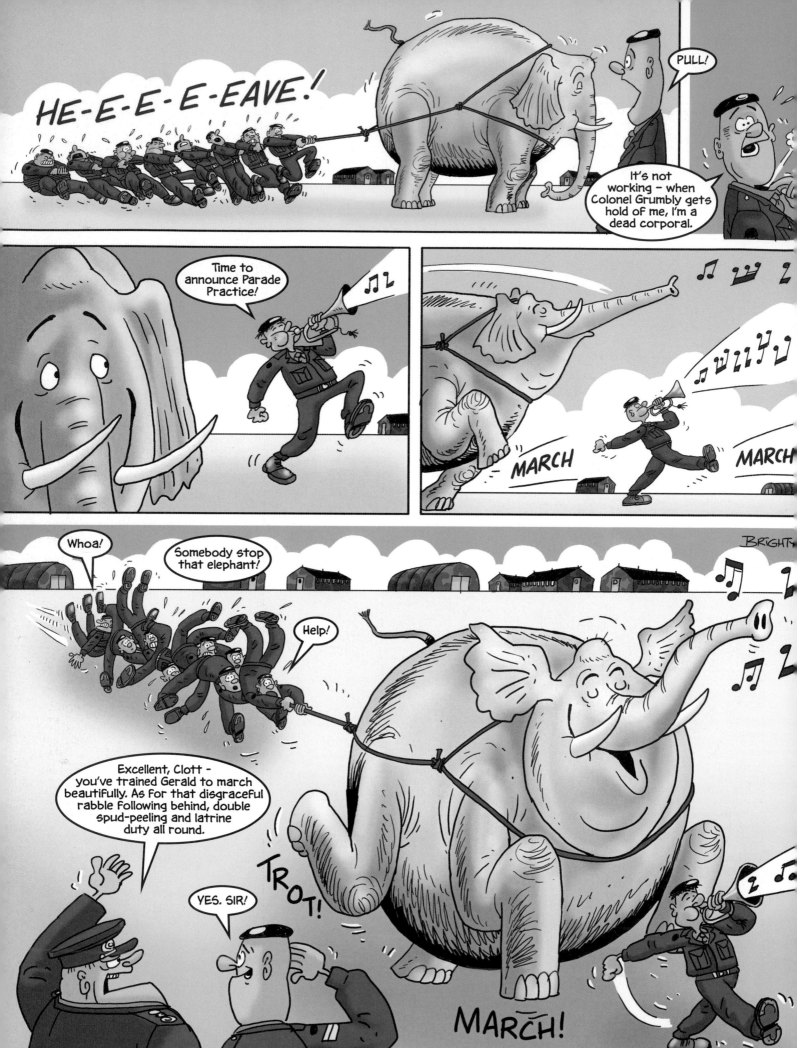

JULIUS SNEEZER THE SNEEZING CAESAR

THE JOCKS AND THE GEORDIES

CROSSPATCH VILLAGE HALL...

Boys, we've tried everything to stop you fighting, and nothing has worked.

But if you promise to train for two weeks instead of fighting, we'll sign you up for the Crosspatch junior boxing tournament!

I'd get to beat up a Geordie in front of his friends and family!

And I'd get a trophy for smacking a Jock!

JUNIOR BOXING TOURNAMENT

That's the spirit!

But remember, no fighting for two whole weeks!

SO...

THUMP! THUMP! THUMP! THUMP! THUMP!

AND...

THUMP! THUMP! THUMP! THUMP! THUMP!

This is wonderful! There's been no scrapping for a whole week!

Maybe this can be a fresh start for the Jocks and the Geordies?

MEANWHILE...

It's those soppy Geordies! Not attacking them isn't natural!

It's the Jocks!

I miss the feeling of their faces against my fists!

Lovely day for a run, isn't it?

Yes! Good luck in the tournament!

I feel ashamed!

PUFF! PANT! GROAN!

I feel sick... and not from the running!

Beryl the Peril

KEYHOLE KATE

BLACK BOB
THE DANDY'S WONDER DOG

Part Three: The Chase Is On!

Black Bob is being chased by two men desperate to conceal secret plans to build a nuclear power station nearby...

1 - The men gave chase in their van. But Bob was strong and fast, and he knew exactly where he was going. For now, he was more than a match for his pursuers. "Come on, Harry - put the foot down," said the foreman. "Don't let him get away with those blueprints, or we're both in big trouble."

2 - "We're gaining on him, Harry," said the foreman. And then, as Bob led them off the main road and into the valley itself, "Mind that hump!" Harry turned a mild shade of green. "That was nearly my lunch!" he exclaimed.

3 - Bob didn't let up, though, and wasn't about to be caught any time soon. But why didn't he head into the fields where the van couldn't follow? Surely that would have made more sense to a smart dog like Bob? But Bob knew these roads, and the bends slowed his pursuers down far more than him, making the chase last longer and longer.

4 - "Keep going, Harry!" urged the foreman. "He's bound to run out of steam soon." But they didn't know Black Bob. There was no fitter and faster hound in the whole of the Scottish Borders, and he was in just the mood to prove it. The question was not when Bob would run out of steam, but...

5 - "When would the van would run out of *diesel*? The answer came soon, but as the van slowed, so too did Bob. Had he finally succumbed to tiredness? "GAH! We've run out of fuel." snarled Harry. "Never mind," said the foreman. "It looks like the mutt has run himself out too. We'll grab the plans and then find help to get us back on the move again."

6 - "Careful, Charlie," warned Harry, as the foreman advanced towards Black Bob. "That dog's got spirit... and teeth." Charlie smiled grimly. "Don't worry about me, Harry - I know how to handle *dumb animals*."

To be continued...

Monkey Bizness

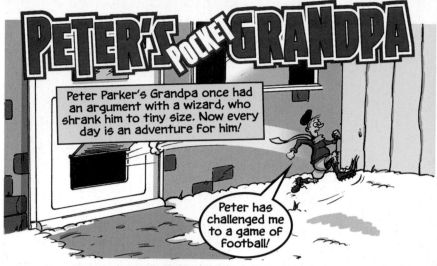

PETER'S POCKET GRANDPA

Peter Parker's Grandpa once had an argument with a wizard, who shrank him to tiny size. Now every day is an adventure for him!

Peter has challenged me to a game of football!

A jog round the block will soon get me warmed up.

PONG!

Not as warm as THAT, though!

Yeeuck! Puff...

Pant...

?

SPLAT!

Bloomin' heck! Who put that monstrosity here?

Well, might as well make the most of it. A bit of mountaineering will get me fit for the game!

I name this mountain...

BULLY BEEF AND CHIPS

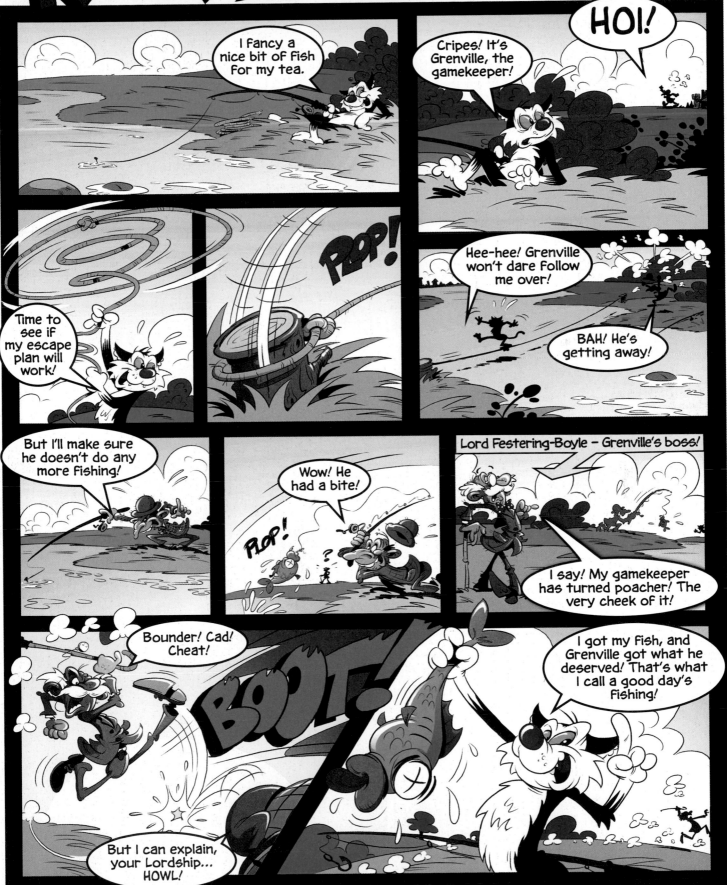

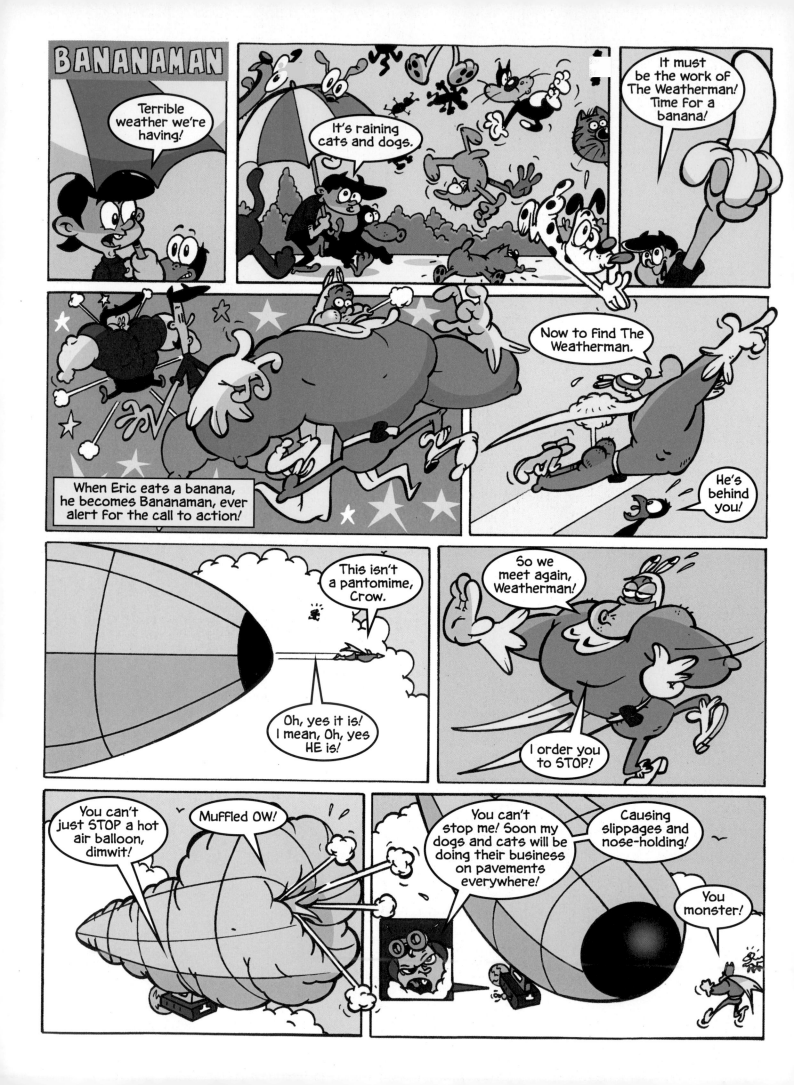

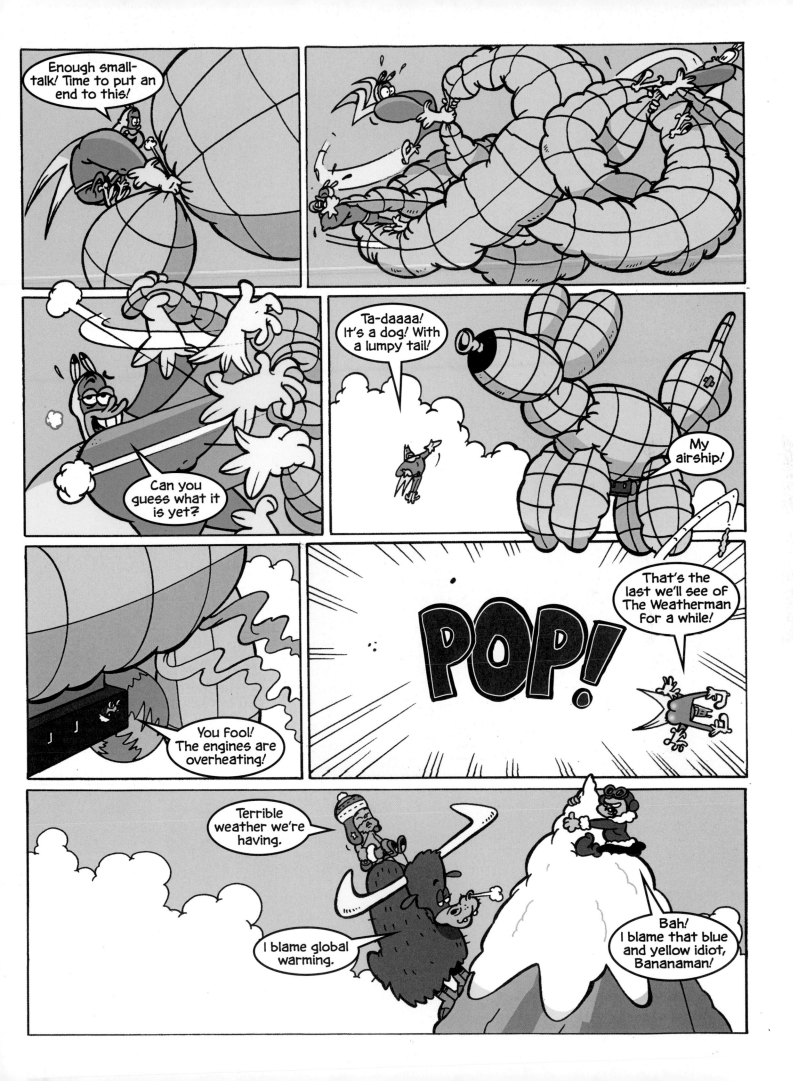

JULIUS SNEEZER — THE SNEEZING CAESAR

Monkey Bizness

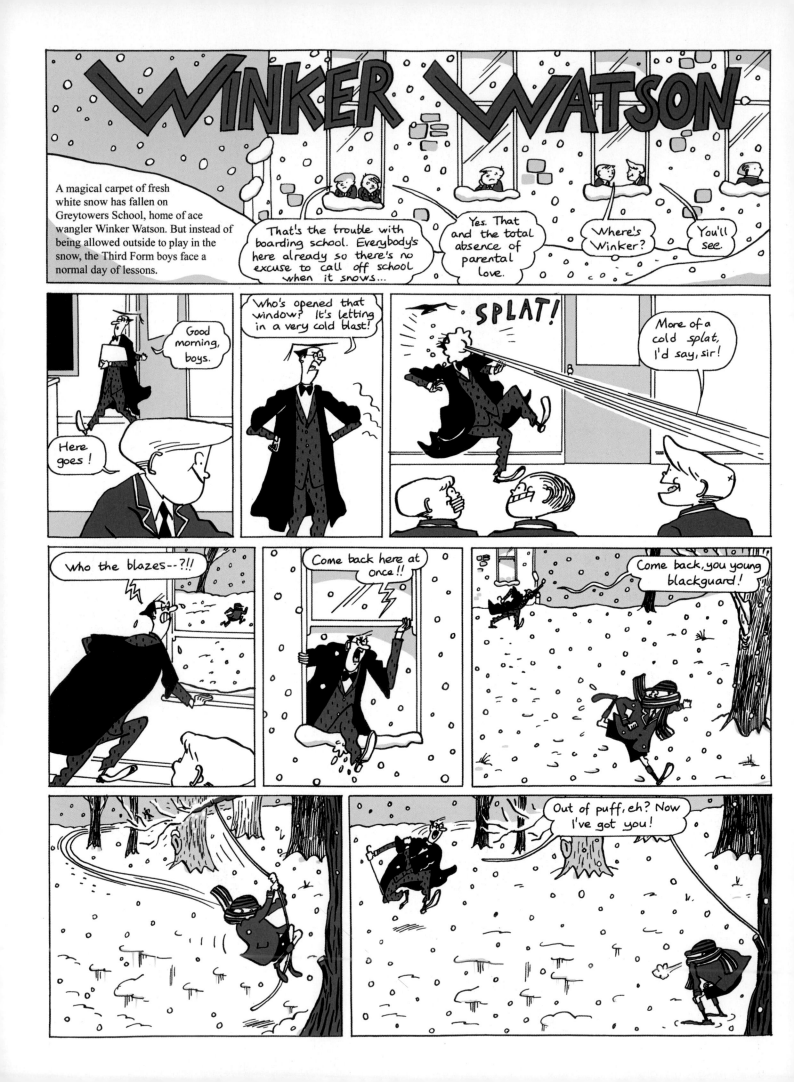

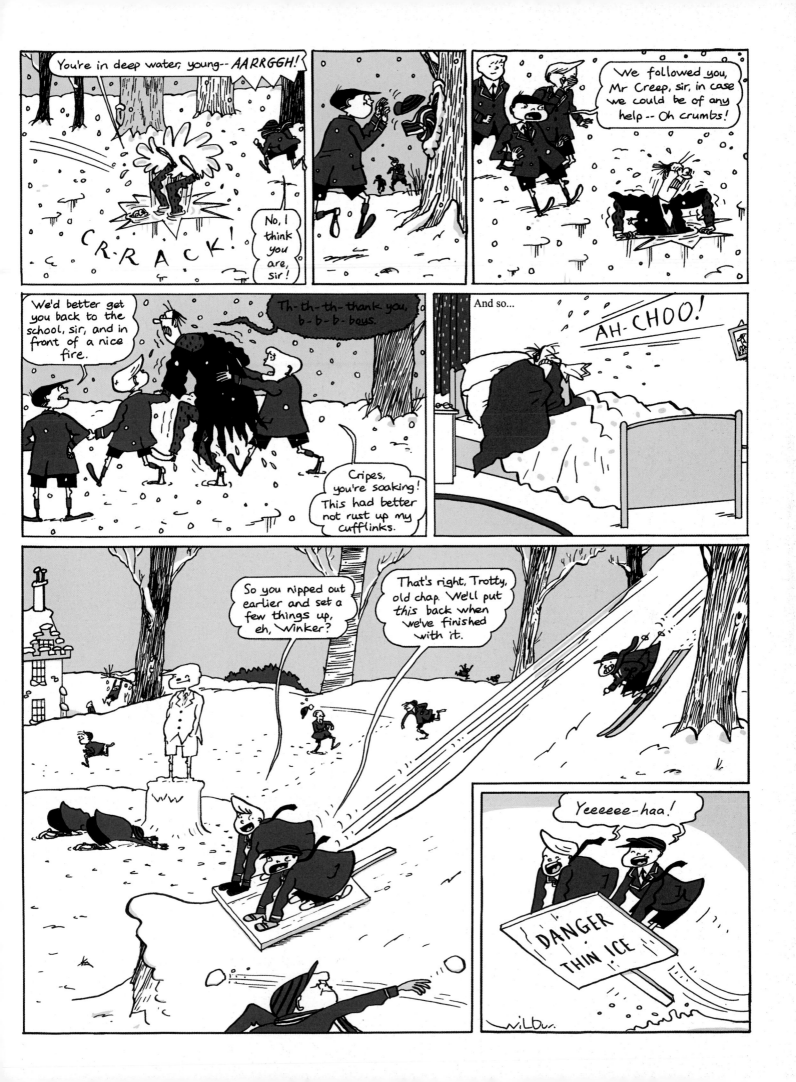

The SMASHER

LEW STRINGER..

KEYHOLE KATE

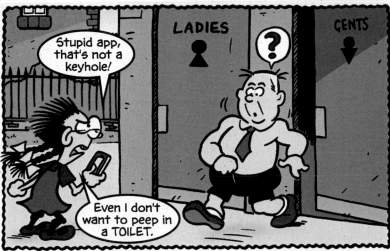

THE BADD LADS

Did you know you can do this just as easily online these days?

If the cops catch us we'll go down for a long time for armed robbery!

But we only ever use *toy* guns... This water pistol isn't even loaded!

That's right, Knuck, but it's still a risky business.

I think that cashier might have something. We'd be better off getting into cyber crime!

Cider crime, Boss? What, you mean scrumping apples?

No, you goof! Cyber crime. Boss is talking about computers.

Cider crime! Ha ha! You are a doofus, sometimes, Knuck!

Hey lads, I've got into cyber crime. I've nicked a computer!

(Sigh) That's not what Boss meant, either, Knucklehead. Cyber crime isn't pinching computers—it's online fraud and stuff.

Yeah, but you do need a computer to do it, Fingers. Good lad, Knuck!

Oh yeah! That's true.

EUREKA!

Sounds like Boss has cracked the cyber crime lark at last!

Are we rich yet, Boss?

Well, no, but I've worked out how to switch the computer on...

Wha--?!

Sometimes you're not so dumb, Knuck. That cyber crime stuff is *hard*.

Yeah! Cider crime is a much better idea!

BRASSNECK

It's Christmas Concert time at Charlie Brand's school...

Fatso Snodgrass, Headmaster.

...and so, without further ado, I give you our first act, the Trumpeteers!

PARP!

HONK!

Bleep! My transistors are rattling, Charlie!

This is going to be a long afternoon.

Opera next...

La burger, la pizza, la kebab... Moan... groan..

Blimey! Brian's NOT got opera talent!

Then rock 'n' roll...

TRIP!

...Rocking around the Christmas Treeeeeaargh!

Bleep! Hit my shutdown button, Charlie.

This is terrible!

The Nativity...

Aaargh!

Women and children first!

Abandon stage!

Bleep! Gotcha, Gordon!

Crumbs, you're heavy! Bleep!

KRASH!

Too heavy for the stage, it seems!

Get back to your seat, you metal miscreant! The show must go on!

Yes, Fatso! I mean yes, Mr Snodgrass!

The concert continues...

Who's up next, Brassneck?

Bleep! Bad news, Charlie!

It's Swotty Watt's violin concerto!

We've got to stop him! Swotty will screech and scrape on his violin for hours!

Almost time for the performance of a lifetime!

Bleep! Got him!

I say! Glurk!

I'll line up an alternative act for Swotty!

Let me out!

What IS that terrible noise, tinhead?

It's my favourite music, Fatso – HEAVY METAL!

Rocking!

Yay!

Awesome!

THE JOCKS AND THE GEORDIES

THE BADD LADS

Scrap metal is getting a good price these days, lads. Let's see if we can pinch some.

Boss! Fingers! I've found some!

Good old Knuck!

Oops!

You swiped the cover off this manhole, didn't you, Knucklehead?

Yes, boss. Sorry, boss.

I've got an idea, Fingers, you come with me. Knuck, see what else you can find.

Okay, Boss.

Later.

Bah. No luck. Now, where are Boss and Fingers? Hey, this ladder's made of metal. Perfect!

Knuck! Come back with our ladder! We're pinching the lead off this roof!

!?

Oh dear.

POLICE

Hmmm... Perhaps we can show our mettle, yet. Fingers, do you think your aunt could make us one of her special cakes?

One with a file in? Sure, Boss.

They've escaped, sarge! And not only that...

They've nicked the bars on the window!

1 - And true to his word, Charlie found that Bob was in no mood to struggle, handing over the cardboard tube without further resistance. The two men could not have been more pleased. "Ha!" laughed Charlie. "What did I tell you, Harry? Putty in my hands. All's well that ends well."

2 - Well, perhaps not quite. This was one "dumb animal" who knew exactly what he was doing. "Oh no! It's EMPTY, Harry!" wailed Charlie. "We're stuck out here in the middle of nowhere, with no fuel ... and no blueprint! Where can it be?"

3 – Thanks to Andrew Glenn's quick thinking, the blueprint was in the office of Douglas McKinley, editor of The Borders Times. "This is outrageous!" stormed McKinley. "We'll launch a campaign against these plans immediately. They can find somewhere else for their ugly, dirty power plant."

4 - And so the campaign began. It raised a furious public outcry from all over Scotland, and plans to build a nuclear power station in the Borders were quietly shelved. A shepherd and his brave, faithful sheepdog had saved their beloved, beautiful valley for generations to come.

5 - Today, sixty years later, the valley remains much the same. Yes, man's needs won out eventually, but a cleaner, more graceful way to tap the valley's resources was found. And that would have made one man and his dog very, very proud.

THE END.

The SMASHER

Take Pongo for a walk, Smasher, but don't try to smash anything or you'll be grounded!

I promise I won't smash a thing, dad!

Heh heh! I won't smash anything, but I can train the dog to do it!

Hold the ladder steady, son, while I paint the house!

Oho!

Fancy a dog biscuit, Pongo?

Ha-ha! Stop! His tail's tickling me!

WAG! WAG!

SMASH!

Time to go!

OOFYA!

WOBBLE!

Later...

Hmm... I wonder what would happen if Pongo saw that squirrel?

PONGO! SQUIRREL! Oops!

CHARGE!

SMASH!

GAHHH! Your dog's just ruined hours of work!

RUN LIKE FUN!

Back home...

I've heard about you training Pongo to be a smasher! You're grounded! Get to your room!

AW, dad!

Hey Pongo! Come back!

BOUND!

SMASH!

BOING!

Oh no! My bed's bust!

CRACK!

And so...

Bah! Looks like I trained you TOO well!

ZZZ...

PONGO

LEW STRINGER..